Reach Out

Advisory Panel
Sharon Adams
Marilyn Bailey
Susan Davis
Sue Evans
Demetra Georgopoulos
Vangie Kalanderopoulos
Nancy Leonard
Linda Miller
Miriam Trehearne

Senior Program Consultant
Jennette MacKenzie

Program Consultant
Christine Finochio

I(T)P Nelson

an International Thomson Publishing company

Toronto • Albany • Bonn • Boston • Cincinnati • Detroit • London • Madrid • Melbourne
Mexico City • New York • Pacific Grove • Paris • San Francisco • Singapore • Tokyo • Washington

I(T)P® International Thomson Publishing

The ITP logo is a trademark under licence
www.thomson.com

© Copyright 1999 ITP®Nelson

Published by

I(T)P® Nelson

A division of Thomson Canada Limited
1120 Birchmount Road
Scarborough, Ontario M1K 5G4
www.nelson.com

Printed and bound in Canada
5 6 7 8 9 0 / ITIB / 7 6 5 4 3 2

Canadian Cataloguing in Publication Data

Main entry under title:

Nelson language arts

Contents: (v.1) Step out – (v.2) Reach out – (v.3) Leap out
ISBN 0-17-618557-7 (v.1) ISBN 0-17-618558-5 (v.2) ISBN 0-17-618559-3 (v.3)

1. Readers (Primary). I. Title: Nelson language arts 2.

PE1119.N443 1998	428.6	C98-932551-2

Executive Editor: Susan Green
Project Editor: Anne-Marie Wallace
Production Coordinator: Theresa Thomas
Art Direction and Design: Liz Harasymczuk
Permissions: Jill Young
Equity Consultant: Ken Ramphal

Table of Contents

Unit 1: You and Me

When you read stories about other people, you think about your own feelings and things that happen to you.

BE A BETTER READER

- read on or read back to look for clues to figure out new words

- use picture clues

- think about what you know

I Am

Written by Nikki Grimes

I laugh
shout
sing
smile
whisper
hum
howl
gurgle
giggle
sigh.

I am
joy.

What's Your Name?

Adapted from What's Your Name? *by Eve Sanders*

A name can be long or short, new or old. It can be borrowed, passed down, or made up from a special word.

> Wherever it comes from,
> Whatever it means,
> Your name is yours,
> To write in big letters or small,
> To whisper or shout,
> To say: here I am …

EVA. My name is for remembering my great-grandma. Her name was Eva, too. In Hebrew, Eva means "life." Every Sunday, my dad and I go someplace: the museum, the park, the beach. I feel happy when I can run with my dad. I drive fast in my wheelchair. I zoom around and explore.

BLAKELY. I looked up my name in a book. Blakely means "from the black meadow." It makes me think of rain and storms. I play volleyball with my mom. My dad said I should learn basketball, too, because I'm going to be tall. So I joined a basketball team called "The Rockets."

FREDRON. Fredron is my father's name, too. I want to be an artist because my grandfather is an artist. I learned to draw from comic books. Now my grandfather is teaching me technique. He showed me how the light changes everything. My eyes are green in the sunshine.

MAGGIE. My mom named me after my grandma Genaille. I'm the only grandchild that is named after her. My grandma raised eleven children and is very strong and brave. One day I hope I can be like her. I feel like I can be anything I want.

MATTHEW. My mom and dad liked the name Matthew. I'm the first person in our family to have that name. I live on a farm and like to help my dad take care of the animals. I want to be a farmer like him when I grow up.

AFTER YOU READ

Find out about your name

Write about your own name. Were you named after someone special?

The Leaving Morning

Written by Angela Johnson
Illustrated by David Soman

READING TIP

Look for clues in pictures

The pictures in a story help you find out what will happen. Look at the pictures before you read.

The Leaving happened on a soupy, misty morning, when you could hear the street sweeper. Sssshhhshsh….

We pressed our faces against the hall window and left cold lips on the pane.

It was the leaving morning.
Boxes of clothes,
toys,
dishes,
and pictures of us everywhere.

The leaving had been long because we'd packed
days before and said goodbye
to everyone we knew....

Our friends....

The grocer....

Everybody in
our building....

And the cousins, especially the cousins.

We said goodbye to the cousins all day long.

Mama said the people in a truck would move us
and take care of everything we loved,
on the leaving morning.

We woke up early and had hot cocoa from the deli
across the street.
I made more lips on the deli window
and watched for the movers on the leaving
morning.

We sat on the steps and
watched the movers.
They had blue moving clothes on
and made bumping noises on the stairs.
There were lots of whistles
and "Watch out, kids."

I sat between my mama and daddy,
holding their hands.
My daddy said in a little while we'd be someplace
we'd love.

So I left lips on the front window of our apartment,
and said goodbye to our old place,
on the leaving morning.

AFTER YOU READ

Think about the story

Did everything happen in the story the way you
thought it would? How did the pictures help
you understand the story?

Violet's Purple World

Written by John McLaughlin
Illustrated by Lynn Jeffery

Violet had a purple house near the shore.
She loved her house and everything about
it. She loved the ocean and she loved the
sand. She loved the rain on her purple tin
roof, and she loved the smell of the fresh,
salty air. She even loved the strong wind
that made her trees grow on a slant.

Violet even dressed her two dogs in little
purple coats to wear in the cold winters.
When she took them for walks, they looked
like two bunches of grapes.

One very stormy night, when the tide was
higher than Violet had ever seen it, the wind
roared in from the ocean. Violet could hear
the waves crashing against the shore. She
heard the sounds of the ocean getting closer
and closer to her little purple house.

All at once, the strong wind banged against Violet's house so hard that it smashed the window beside her. Then, with a great burst and a loud bang, the front door blew open and a stream of ocean water began to trickle onto Violet's purple carpet.

Violet was afraid.

Violet picked up her two dogs and dashed out
the door. She ran through the icy water that
soaked right through her purple slippers. She
climbed the hill behind her house and
walked sadly along the road. Her neighbour's
house sat on higher ground and was safe
from the terrible tide.

The next day, when the storm was over,
Violet walked back down the hill. Purple tin
sheets from her roof were scattered all over
the yard. Purple boards were hanging off the
side of the house. Violet's beautiful purple
quilt had blown out of the window and was
caught in one of the slanted trees.

Violet's dogs ran ahead of her into the house. When Violet looked inside, she saw them standing in water up to their bellies. She sat down in the water and put her head in her hands. But not for long. Violet took a deep breath.

She found her scissors in the kitchen drawer and cut the sleeves off her purple sweater. Then she dressed each of her dogs in a warm purple sleeve.

"There," said Violet. "Dry dogs!"

Violet walked through the field on the hill behind her house. Then she picked some purple violets and held them to her face. She ran back to her house.

She found a bottle for the purple violets and placed them on top of the table.

When she looked at her purple flowers, Violet's troubles didn't seem so great any more. The water didn't seem so cold. She thought she would make some new curtains to replace the old wet ones, maybe some white curtains with bright purple polka dots.

All of a sudden, she heard the dogs barking outside.

Violet looked out the window and saw a crowd of people walking down the hill. Some carried mops and some carried shovels, some carried pails and some carried food.
Mrs. McKinnon, who lived next door, was swinging her tool kit in one hand and her hammer in the other.

"Hello, Violet!" shouted Mrs. McKinnon. "We've come to help you clean up!"

Violet called to them. "Thank you all," she said,
and she picked up her own shovel and started to
scoop the sand off her verandah.

One by one, each of her friends began to help. Mrs.
McKinnon fixed the purple boards that hung from
the side of the house. Mr. Wong climbed onto the
roof and replaced the purple tin sheets. Before long,
all of Violet's friends were busy helping to bring her
little home back to life.

Violet smiled as she continued working, and little
by little, her battered house became beautifully
purple once again.

Dear Neighbours,

Purple curtains
Purple nets
Purple chairs and purple pets.
Purple cookies
Made with oats
Purple oars for purple boats.
Purple shovels
Moving sand
Neighbours lend a purple hand.
Purple evenings
Purple lights
Purple stars on purple kites.
Purple flowers
Touched with dew
Purple Violet's dream come true.

Thank you from Violet

AFTER YOU READ

Make a list

Write three new words you read in the story. How did you figure out what they mean?

Helping Hands

Alexander and the Terrible, Horrible, No Good, Very Bad Day

Written by Judith Viorst
Illustrated by Ray Cruz

READING TIP

Think about what you know

When you have a bad day, how do you feel? As you read, think about how Alexander's feelings are like yours.

I went to sleep with gum in my mouth and now there's gum in my hair and when I got out of bed this morning I tripped on the skateboard and by mistake I dropped my sweater in the sink while the water was running and I could tell it was going to be a terrible, horrible, no good, very bad day.

At breakfast Anthony found a Corvette Sting Ray car kit in his breakfast cereal box and Nick found a Junior Undercover Agent code ring in his breakfast cereal box but in my breakfast cereal box all I found was breakfast cereal.

I think I'll move to Australia.

In the car pool Mrs. Gibson let Becky have a seat by the window. Audrey and Elliott got seats by the window too. I said I was being scrunched. I said I was being smushed. I said, if I don't get a seat by the window I am going to be carsick. No one even answered.

I could tell it was going to be a terrible, horrible, no good, very bad day.

At school Mrs. Dickens liked Paul's picture of the sailboat better than my picture of the invisible castle.

At singing time she said I sang too loud. At counting time she said I left out sixteen. Who needs sixteen?

I could tell it was going to be a terrible, horrible, no good, very bad day.

I could tell because Paul said I wasn't his best friend anymore. He said that Philip Parker was his best friend and that Albert Moyo was his next best friend and that I was only his third best friend.

I hope you sit on a tack, I said to Paul. I hope the next time you get a double-decker strawberry ice-cream cone the ice cream part falls off the cone part and lands in Australia.

There were two cupcakes in Philip Parker's lunch bag and Albert got a Hershey bar with almonds and Paul's mother gave him a piece of jelly roll that had little coconut sprinkles on the top. Guess whose mother forgot to put in dessert?

It was a terrible, horrible, no good, very bad day.

That's what it was, because after school my mom
took us all to the dentist and Dr. Fields found a
cavity just in me. Come back next week and I'll fix
it, said Dr. Fields.

Next week, I said, I'm going to Australia.

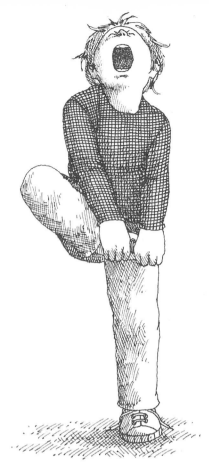

On the way downstairs the elevator door closed on my foot and while we were waiting for my mom to go get the car Anthony made me fall where it was muddy and then when I started crying because of the mud Nick said I was a crybaby and while I was punching Nick for saying crybaby my mom came back with the car and scolded me for being muddy and fighting.

I am having a terrible, horrible, no good, very bad day, I told everybody. No one even answered.

So then we went to the shoestore to buy some
sneakers. Anthony chose white ones with blue
stripes. Nick chose red ones with white stripes. I
chose blue ones with red stripes but then the shoe
man said, We're all sold out. They made me buy
plain old white ones, but they can't make me wear
them.

When we picked up my dad at his office he said I couldn't play with his copying machine, but I forgot. He also said to watch out for the books on his desk, and I was careful as could be except for my elbow. He also said don't fool around with his phone, but I think I called Australia. My dad said please don't pick him up anymore.

It was a terrible, horrible, no good, very bad day.

There were lima beans for dinner and I hate limas.
There was kissing on TV and I hate kissing.

My bath was too hot, I got soap in my eyes, my
marble went down the drain, and I had to wear my
railroad-train pajamas. I hate my railroad-train
pajamas.

When I went to bed Nick took back the pillow he said I could keep and the Mickey Mouse night light burned out and I bit my tongue.

The cat wants to sleep with Anthony, not with me.

It has been a terrible, horrible, no good, very bad day.

My mom says some days are like that.

Even in Australia.

AFTER YOU READ

Alike and different

How was Alexander's bad day the same as a bad day you have had? How was it different?

You and Me

You have read stories about other children and what happened to them. Think about something that has happened to you. Share it with others by writing a story of your own.

Plan

Stories about you will have words like **I** and **my**.

Think about:
- What happened first?
- What happened next?
- How did you feel?
- Who will read the story?

Make a story map.

Who	Where
What happened?	
1.	
2.	
3.	
How does this story end?	

Write your story

Revise

Read your story.
Pick:

- one thing you liked.
- one thing you didn't like.
- one thing you could make better.

Remember to write an interesting opening sentence to "hook" the reader.

Check

Check your story for spelling and capitals.

Here's how Julien's story started.

> The Day I Moved
>
> One morning I woke up and went downstairs. I saw the moving truck. I remembered this was the day I was moving. I put all my toys in a box. After, I put my games in another box.

Share

Read your story to the class or someone special.

Unit 2: Media Works

There are many different kinds of messages. You will read about messages in advertising, postcards, pictures, and news stories.

BE A BETTER READER

- look at headings
- get information from pictures
- learn parts of a news story

Advertise It!

Written by Mark Cressman
Illustrated by Norman Eyolfson

When you eat your Crunchies
Do you pick them one by one?
Do you grab them by the handful?
Lick your fingers when you're done?
Do you sit and eat them slowly?
Or take the box and run?
No matter how you eat them,
They make breakfast much more fun!

Postcard Messages

Written by Linda Granfield
Illustrated by Ann Iosa

READING TIP

Read headings to find out

Before you read, look at the headings. Headings tell you what you will learn about.

Messages and Postcards

For more than one hundred years, people have been sending messages on postcards. Millions of them have been printed on paper, leather, wood, and even metal. They've been mailed to places all over the world and saved as souvenirs in special scrapbook albums.

Want to join the fun? You can use postcards to
- keep in touch with pen pals
- send a quick note to your grandparents
- celebrate holidays
- remember a family vacation
- share camp experiences with friends

Postcards Old and New

The first postcards were printed in Europe more than 200 years ago. They were used for advertising.

As people began to have more time to travel, they wanted to buy something to remember the places they visited. They would buy souvenirs, including postcards, wherever they went.

Today, there are electronic postcards available on the Internet. You can visit sites around the world, and trade cards with other collectors.

Travel Cards

Whether you buy them or make your own, postcards are a great record of your vacation trip. Each year, new postcard designs and pictures are made. There are at least 5000 different postcard views of Niagara Falls!

Fun with Travel Cards

- Mail a postcard to a friend. You can share your new experiences and stay in touch.
- Make an album and put postcards in it. You'll have something to bring back memories for years to come.
- Collect cards of your hometown. Make a postcard of your city for someone who has never been there.

- Send a pen pal a postcard of your house, even your bedroom (before and after you cleaned it up!).
- Invent an imaginary place. Create a map postcard of that place. How many details can you include?

Postcards of the Past, Present, and Future

Old postcards show us how people lived long ago. We see how they dressed, where they lived, and what they did to have fun. Famous people appeared on postcards the way rock singers and movie stars appear on posters today. Sometimes the postcards were the only pictures the fans ever saw.

Collecting Postcards

Once you begin finding and keeping old postcards, or making and using your original designs, you've become a "deltiologist" (pronounced DEL-tee-ol-o-gist), or a postcard collector! You'll want to keep the postcards your friends send, and old cards you've found, in a special place … like a postcard album.

AFTER YOU READ

Find important ideas

Write down each heading. Under each heading write one thing you learned.

Pictures Talk

Written by Susan Green

READING TIP

Get information from pictures

Pictures give you information. Look at the pictures before you read. What does each picture tell you?

This picture reminds people of a special celebration.

We all like to look at pictures. We have pictures of our family and friends. We take pictures of special places and to remember special times.

People work to clean up the environment.

When you look at a magazine or newspaper, the pictures and words work together to tell you about what is happening in your community and the world. Sometimes a picture can even tell a story by itself.

An ice storm brings down hydro wires.

The Canadarm is used in space by a shuttle crew.

Pictures help you understand what is happening in the news. They help you to see what an event was like and how it must have felt to be there.

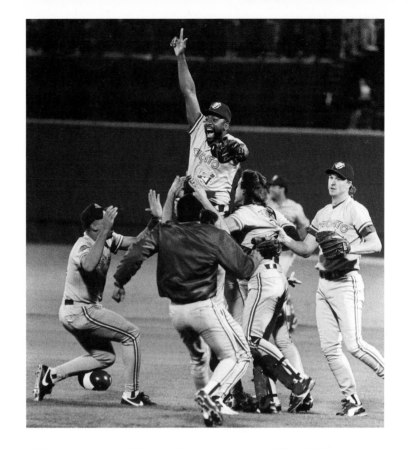

The Toronto Blue Jays win the World Series.

From magazines and newspapers, to TV and the Internet, pictures everywhere tell us about the world we live in and make us feel a part of it.

AFTER YOU READ

Make a web

Make a web. Put the word "pictures" in the middle and write what you learned about pictures around it.

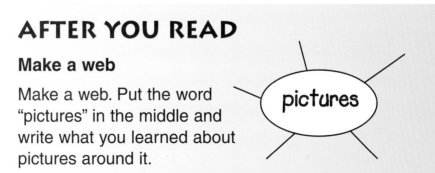

In the News

Written by Robert Cutting
Illustrated by Capucine Mazille

Who **Where** **Why** **What** **When**

When you read a newspaper story, there are five things to look for. A good news story will tell you who it is about, what it is about, where it happened, when it happened, and why it happened.

Here is an example of a story that answers these five questions.

Dog Finds His Way Home

On August 15, Mr. and Mrs. Chan and their children Laura, 7, and Edmund, 8, moved from Vancouver to Ladner. Their dog Pal is a beagle with a bushy tail. He had become friendly with the movers. Mr. and Mrs. Chan said Pal could ride with the movers to Ladner.

The family left their old home in Vancouver at 11:00 a.m. The movers were right behind.

At 12:30, everyone arrived at the new house. The Chans went to get Pal. He wasn't with the movers. There had been a mix-up. The movers thought Pal was with the two children in the car.

Mr. Chan and the movers started to unpack. Mrs. Chan and the children went searching for Pal. "We drove back to Vancouver," she said. "We thought he might still be at the old house."

But Pal wasn't there. After three hours, Mrs. Chan drove back to Ladner.

Meanwhile, Pal had been seen by several people. A police officer reported that she saw a beagle with a bushy tail. It was seen on Granville Street. On August 16, a taxi driver called into his office. He had seen a "different looking dog" in Richmond. On August 17, two bus drivers reported seeing a "cute beagle" running along Highway 99.

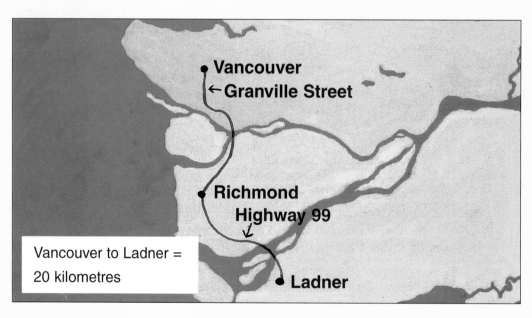

Vancouver
←Granville Street

Richmond
Highway 99

Ladner

Vancouver to Ladner = 20 kilometres

Mr. Sikundar, a Vancouver ambulance driver explained how he saw a dog run right by his ambulance on August 18. "It looked like a beagle," said Mr. Sikundar.

Finally, at 9:00 p.m. on August 18, Laura Chan heard a scratch at the front door. When she opened it, there sat Pal. He was panting and wagging his tail. The whole family crowded around their dog. Somehow, Pal had found his way to his new home!

AFTER YOU READ

Make a chart

Make a chart with the headings Who, What, When, Where, Why. Fill in the answers you read in the news story.

Media Works

You read about different media and the messages they send. Think about something that happened to you or someone else and tell your own news story in a picture with a caption.

Plan

Think about the 5 W's.
- How can you show your story in a picture?
- What will your caption say?

What

Who

Where

5 W's

Why

When

Draw your picture and write your caption

Revise

Work with a partner. Ask them to look at your picture and caption. Here are some things they might say:

- I liked the part where you...
- One thing you could change is...
- Tell me more about...
- You could add...

Luca wrote this caption for his picture.
The first place dog in the city dog show is a Siberian husky named Jessie.

Check

Check your caption for spelling and punctuation.

Share

Create a class bulletin board for the news pictures and captions.

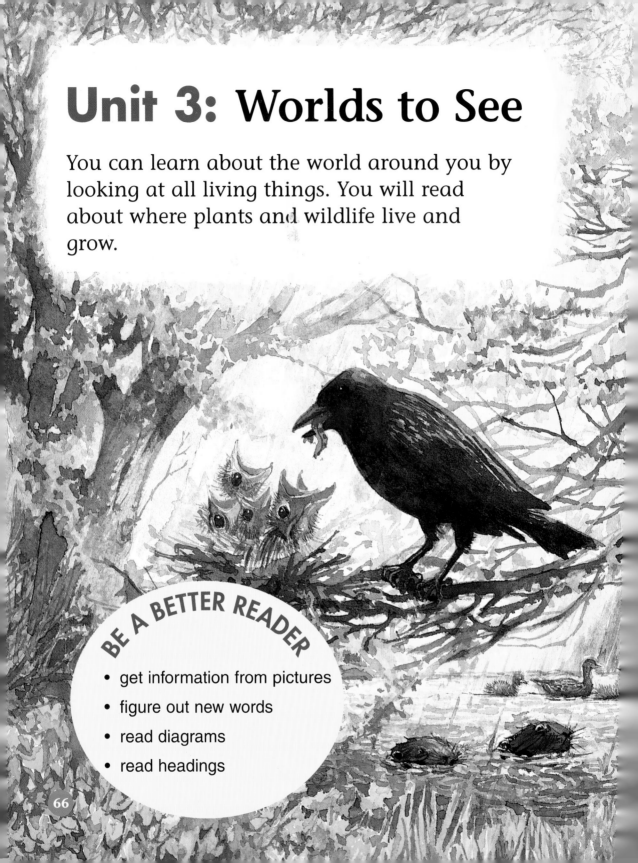

Unit 3: Worlds to See

You can learn about the world around you by looking at all living things. You will read about where plants and wildlife live and grow.

BE A BETTER READER

- get information from pictures
- figure out new words
- read diagrams
- read headings

The Gifts of Spring

Written by Jan Bourdeau Waboose
Illustrated by Eric Copeland

S is for the smell of Sweetgrass
P is for the Pond where the baby beavers play
R is for the cool Rain that plants and trees will drink
I is for ME RUNNING EVERYWHERE
N is for the Nest of the baby crows
G is for the Gifts of Spring.

©OPELAND

Window Watcher

Written by Lynne Kepler
Illustrated by Stephen Quinlan

READING TIP

Get information from headings and pictures

Before you read, look at the headings and pictures.
They will give you information about the selection.

Did you know you can find out about many things just by looking out the window? You might want to try looking for different kinds of information outside the window in your classroom.

Seasons

How can you tell what season it is? Check the colour of the leaves, what people are wearing, or whether it is raining or snowing.

Temperature

What is the temperature outside? There are clues all around you. You can use a thermometer to record the temperature in a graph. You can look at what people are doing and wearing.

Birds

What kinds of birds live around you? You can place feeder trays outside your window. Then watch what kinds of birds come to the feeder, the times of day they come, and whether they share with other birds.

Clouds

What can clouds tell you? Look out the window to see what kinds of clouds are in the sky and draw the different kinds of clouds you see. You can keep a chart to show which kinds of clouds go with different kinds of weather.

Shapes

What shapes can you spot outside your window? You can look for shapes in nature or shapes in buildings. Your school will have its own shapes too—inside and in the schoolyard.

What other things can you learn about by being a "window watcher"? All year long a window can be a way to learn about and observe the world around you.

AFTER YOU READ

Write a sentence

Write a sentence to tell how the headings and pictures helped you read.

The Great Swamp

Written by Kiera Schneider as told to Dan Schneider

READING TIP

Read new words

When you come to a word you don't know, read
the rest of the sentence to find clues.

Hi! I'm Kiera, and I'm eight years old. This spring
break, my sister, Sophie, who's only six, my mom
and dad and I took a holiday in a swamp. But this
was no ordinary swamp. We drove all the way from
our home in Puslinch, Ontario, to the Okefenokee
Swamp in southern Georgia. We arrived after dark,
and the swamp looked very spooky and really
mysterious.

The next morning, we met Ranger Pete, who took us out in his boat to explore the wildlife refuge. He told us that swamps aren't as scary as most people imagine. Even the alligators aren't dangerous, he said, if you leave them alone and keep at least six metres away from them. Ranger Pete should know, because he's been an Okefenokee guide for 10 years.

Later that afternoon, we went for a walk in the woods. Something rustled under the leaves. A big snake! Sophie and I jumped back, but Ranger Pete explained it was a grey rat snake and it wasn't poisonous like the diamondback rattlesnakes and cottonmouths that also live there. He picked up the snake and let me hold it. Its skin was smooth and dry, not slimy as I thought it would be.

On our second night, we left our warm sleeping
bags and went on a swamp prowl. I wasn't really
scared, but the shadows were a little creepy, and I
was glad my mom and dad were there. We saw a
little grey fox scurry by, sniffing around for food.
Out in the water, alligator eyes shone like reddish-
orange coals in our flashlight beams.

Then we heard a loud commotion; it sounded like a parade marching through the woods! Following our dad, we crept closer to the noise. Sophie spotted it first—one of the weirdest animals we had ever seen.

It looked like a walking rock, about the size of a football. We looked closer and saw that the "rock" had giant claws, a long, thin snout, and a hard shell made of huge overlapping plates. It was an armadillo!

On our last day, we took one last canoe trip and found an alligator on a tiny island. The whole island shook, and the alligator rocked up and down as if it was on a waterbed! The island was floating. We remembered that Ranger Pete told us Okefenokee means "land of the trembling earth" in a Native American language. I guess we found out the hard way how it got its wonderful name.

AFTER YOU READ

Think about your learning

Choose three new words you learned in the story. Write what each word means and what clues you used to figure it out.

What Good Is a Swamp?

Adapted from Wild *magazine*
Illustrated by Steve Attoe

Lots of people think that swamps aren't any
good at all. You can't farm or build houses on
them, and if you tried to cross one in a car or on
a bicycle, you'd probably get stuck. Since they
can't be tamed, people have tried to get rid of
swamps by draining them. It seems some people
just don't understand how important swamps
are to the rest of the planet.

Swamps are great places for wildlife. Frogs, toads, salamanders, fish, otters, beavers, muskrats, alligators, and turtles all live in swamps. Birds nest in trees and find lots of food below—insects, salamanders, frogs, and fish.

Have you ever visited a swamp? What kinds of wildlife lived there?

rain

release moisture

But swamps are good for people too. When it rains, swamps suck up water like a giant sponge. This helps stop floods that can wreck homes and damage cities! Swamps hold the rain and runoff, releasing it slowly when the weather is really dry.

The bottom line: swamps are important—both to animals and to us!

AFTER YOU READ

Draw a picture

Tell how the pictures helped you read. Choose one new thing you learned. Draw a picture to help you remember the information.

Frog Time

Written by Sue Ann Alderson
Illustrated by Ann Blades

Spring song: frog spawn.
Eggs hatch: a crowd of tadpoles on the go.
Tails shrink, legs and lungs grow.

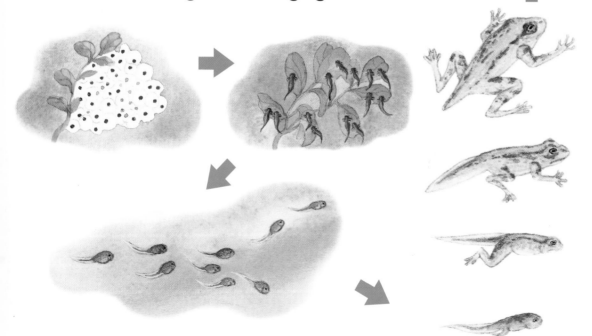

Froglets on land leapfrog about,
see sky, catch dinner on the fly,
sing frog songs long and loud!

AFTER YOU READ

Think about your learning

How did the arrows help you figure out how the
frog changes as it grows.

The Salamander Room

Written by Anne Mazer
Illustrated by Steve Johnson and Lou Fancher

READING TIP

Think like an author

Some authors put facts in the stories they write. As you read, look for information the author puts in the story about salamanders.

Brian found a salamander in the woods. It was a little orange salamander that crawled through the dried leaves of the forest floor.

The salamander was warm and cozy in the boy's hand. "Come live with me," Brian said.

He took the salamander home.

"Where will he sleep?" his mother asked.

"I will make him a salamander bed to sleep in.
I will cover him with leaves that are fresh and
green, and bring moss that looks like little stars to
be a pillow for his head. I will bring him crickets to
sing him to sleep and bullfrogs to tell him good-
night stories."

"And when he wakes up, where will he play?"

"I will carpet my room with shiny wet leaves and water them so he can slide around and play.

I will bring tree stumps into my room so he can climb up the bark and sun himself on top. And I will bring boulders that he can creep over."

"He will miss his friends in the forest."

"I will bring salamander friends to play with him."

"They will be hungry. How will you feed them?"

"I will bring insects to live in my room. And every day I will catch some and feed the salamanders. And I will make little pools of water on top of the boulders so they can drink whenever they are thirsty."

"The insects will multiply, and soon there will be bugs and insects everywhere."

"I will find birds to eat the extra bugs and insects. And the bullfrogs will eat them too."

"Where will the birds and bullfrogs live?"

"I will bring trees for the birds to roost in, and make ponds for the frogs."

"Birds need to fly."

"We can lift off the ceiling. They will sail out in the sky, but they will come back to my room when it is time for dinner, because they will know that the biggest, juiciest insects are there."

"But the trees—how will they grow?"

"The rain will come through the open roof, and the sun, too. And vines will creep up the walls of my room, and ferns will grow under my bed. There will be big white mushrooms and moss like little stars growing around the tree stumps that the salamanders climb on."

"And you—where will you sleep?"

"I will sleep on a bed under the stars, with the moon shining through the green leaves of the trees; owls will hoot and crickets will sing; and next to me, on the boulder with its head resting on soft moss, the salamander will sleep."

AFTER YOU READ

Write facts

Write three facts you learned about salamanders in this story.

Make a Terrarium

Written by Lizann Flatt
Illustrated by Bart Vallecoccia

READING TIP

Use action words

Action words make it easier to understand directions. As you read, look for the action word in each step.

You can bring a bit of the outdoors inside with this garden in glass.

What you need:

- a large clear box or jar (an aquarium, fish bowl, or plastic storage box)
- a round plastic container
- gravel or small pebbles
- dirt or potting soil
- plants (dandelions, grass, clover)
- moss, leaves, sticks, bits of bark, stones
- plastic wrap
- water

What to do:

1. Cover the bottom of the large box or jar with gravel or small pebbles.

2. Place the small plastic container in your terrarium for a pond. Leave the lid on loosely.

3. Spread the soil over the pebbles and around the pond. It should be as deep as your middle finger. Pat the dirt down lightly.

4. For each plant, dig a small hole in the soil. Put the plant's roots in the hole. Cover the roots with soil and press the soil down.

5. Now decorate your garden with sticks, bark, stones, leaves, and moss. What would you like to crawl over or hide under if you were living here?

6. Sprinkle water all over the soil so it is damp. Take the lid off the pond and fill it with water.

7. Cover the top of the terrarium with plastic wrap. Poke a few small holes in the plastic with a toothpick or fork.

8. Keep your terrarium near a window, but not in the sun. Sprinkle water on the soil as it dries out and change any old leaves or dying plants with fresh ones.

AFTER YOU READ

Think like an author

What action words did the author use? What else did the author do to help you read the directions?

Worlds to See

You have read information and stories about the environment. Be an information detective and find out about something in your environment.

Ideas

- clouds
- bird
- insect
- tree

Plan

Make a
Know-Wonder-Learn chart.

Anne made a chart about the opossum.

What do I already know?	What do I wonder about?	What did I learn?
• looks like a big mouse • it has whiskers • it hangs upside down by its tail	• where does it live? • what does it eat?	

Find out

1. Look for answers. Use the library, CD-ROMs, or ask an expert.
2. Write only the information that answers your questions.

When you look for answers in books, check the Table of Contents or the Index first.

What do I already know?	What do I wonder about?	What did I learn?
• looks like a big mouse • it has whiskers • it hangs upside down by its tail	• where does it live? • what does it eat?	• it lives in parks and woods • it eats insects, fruit, and plants • babies live in the mother's pouch

Check

Here are some questions to ask yourself:

- Did I answer each question?
- Did I spell special words correctly?
- Did I tell where I found my information?

Share

Make a Let's Find Out centre. Let others read what you found out about your environment.

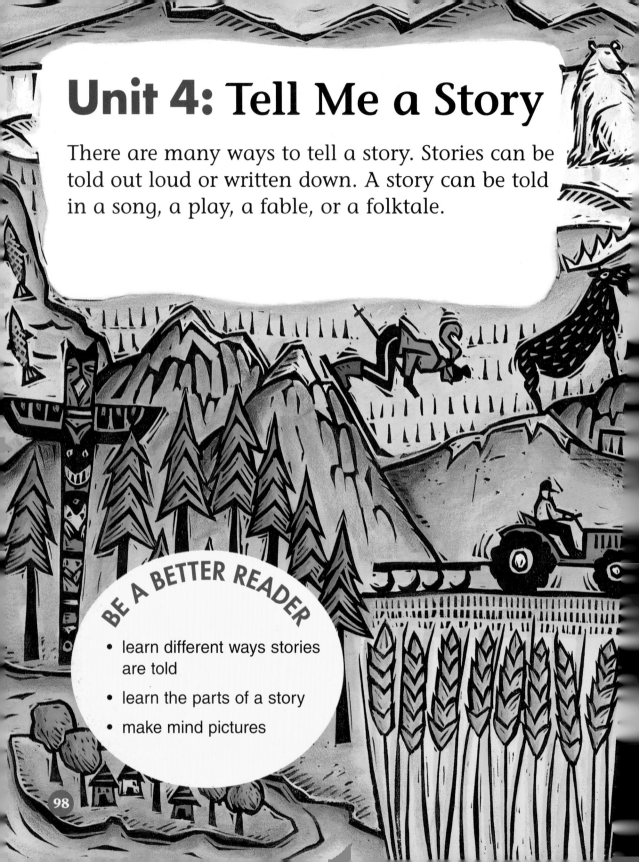

Unit 4: Tell Me a Story

There are many ways to tell a story. Stories can be told out loud or written down. A story can be told in a song, a play, a fable, or a folktale.

BE A BETTER READER

- learn different ways stories are told
- learn the parts of a story
- make mind pictures

This Land is Your Land

Illustrated by Susan Todd

This land is your land
This land is my land
From Bonavista
To Vancouver Island,
From the Arctic Circle,
To the Great Lake waters,
This land was made for you and me

The Three Billy Goats Gruff

Retold by Norma Kennedy
Illustrated by Blanche Sims

READING TIP

Read a play

A play is one way to tell a story. As you read, look
at how the author tells the actors what to do and say.

NARRATOR: Once upon a time, three billy goats
lived together on a hillside. Their names were
Big Billy Goat Gruff, Middle Billy Goat Gruff,
and Little Billy Goat Gruff.

NARRATOR: A river ran beside the billy goats' field, and one day they decided to cross it and eat the grass on the other side. But first they had to go over the bridge, and under the bridge lived a great ugly troll.

(Little Billy Goat Gruff steps onto the bridge)

NARRATOR: *TRIP TRAP* went his hooves.

TROLL *(roaring)*: Who's that tripping over my bridge?

LITTLE BILLY GOAT GRUFF *(in a small voice)*: It is only I, Little Billy Goat Gruff, going across the river to eat the grass on the other side.

TROLL *(fiercely)*: Now I'm coming to gobble you up.

LITTLE BILLY GOAT GRUFF *(timidly)*: Oh, please don't eat me, Troll. I'm so small. Wait for the next billy goat. He's much bigger.

TROLL *(in a mean voice)*: Well, be off with you.

(Middle Billy Goat Gruff steps onto the bridge)

NARRATOR: A little while later, Middle Billy Goat Gruff stepped onto the bridge. *TRIP TRAP, TRIP TRAP* went his hooves.

TROLL *(roaring)*: Who's that tripping over my bridge?

MIDDLE BILLY GOAT GRUFF *(in a bigger voice)*: It is only I, Middle Billy Goat Gruff, going across the river to eat the grass on the other side.

TROLL *(in a mean voice)*: Now I'm coming to gobble you up.

MIDDLE BILLY GOAT GRUFF *(bravely)*: Oh, no, don't eat me. Wait for the next billy goat. He's the biggest of all.

TROLL *(in a meaner voice)*: Very well, be off with you.

(Big Billy Goat Gruff steps onto the bridge)

NARRATOR: It wasn't long before Big Billy Goat Gruff stepped onto the bridge. *TRIP TRAP, TRIP TRAP, TRIP TRAP* went his hooves, and the bridge groaned under his weight.

TROLL *(roaring)*: Who's that tramping over my
　　bridge?

BIG BILLY GOAT GRUFF *(in a big, roaring voice)*: It is
　　I, Big Billy Goat Gruff.

TROLL *(shouting)*: Now I'm coming to gobble you up!

(Troll jumps onto bridge, horrible and hungry)

NARRATOR: But Big Billy Goat Gruff was very fierce and strong. He put down his head and charged the Troll and butted him so hard he flew high into the air and then fell down, down, down, *splash* into the middle of the river.

(Big Billy Goat Gruff butts Troll and Troll falls off bridge)

NARRATOR: And the great ugly troll was never seen again.

NARRATOR: Then Big Billy Goat Gruff joined
Middle Billy Goat Gruff and Little Billy Goat
Gruff in the field on the far side of the river.
They ate so much grass they could hardly walk
home again.

So *snip, snap, snout,* this tale's told out!

AFTER YOU READ

Make a chart

Look back at the play and make a chart of the
things the author does to tell the actors what to do.

The Fable of the Three Frogs

Retold by Carole Spray
Illustrated by Joe Weissmann

READING TIP

Read a fable

A fable is a story that has a lesson. As you read, look for the lesson in the story.

While I was visiting at a farmhouse, I was asked to fetch a kettle full of water at the spring. When I walked down, I discovered this big, wooden cream pail sitting there beside the spring. It was full of cream, but the cover was off. Sitting beside the creamer were three little frogs. They were croaking away, just as happy as they could be.

When the frogs saw me, they jumped. And they jumped so high, all three of them landed in the creamer. I watched them to see what they would do.

They splashed and kicked and thrashed around, but they couldn't seem to get out. Finally, two of them decided it was hopeless. They both gave up trying and clung to the side of the pail.

But the third frog kept at it. She paddled and churned and paddled some more. The cream got thicker and thicker. Finally, she paddled such a long time that a pat of butter started to form on top of the cream. The frog climbed up on the chunk of butter, and gave a mighty hop and got out.

Moral:
If you try hard enough and long enough,
you'll get the job done.

AFTER YOU READ

Think about your learning

In your own words, write what the lesson of the fable is.

The Name of the Tree

Retold by Celia Barker Lottridge
Illustrated by Ian Wallace

READING TIP

Think about the parts of a story

Stories have a beginning, a middle, and an end.
As you read each part, you learn more and more
about the story.

Once, long ago, in the land of the short grass, there was a great hunger. No rain fell, and no grass grew.

All the animals were hungry. They searched in the jungle, they searched by the river, they searched on the great flat plain, but they could find nothing to eat.

At last all the animals gathered together and they said, "Let us go together across the great flat plain until we come to something we can eat."

And so all the animals, except for the lion, who was king and lived in the jungle, walked across the flat, empty land. They walked and walked. After many days, they saw a small bump on the edge of the flat land.

Then they saw that the small bump was a tree. And the tree was very tall. And the tree had fruit on it, such fruit as they had never seen before.

It was as red as pomegranates, as yellow as bananas, as green as melons, as purple as plums, as orange as mangos, and it smelled like all the fruits of the world.

But the tree was so tall and the branches so high that even the giraffe couldn't reach the fruit. And the trunk was so smooth that even the monkey couldn't climb the tree.

The animals sat on the ground and cried because the fruit smelled so good and they were so hungry. At last, when they were too tired to cry any longer, a very old tortoise spoke.

"O animals," she said, "my great-great-great-grandmother told me a story about a wonderful tree. The fruit of that tree was delicious and good to eat. But it could be reached only by those who knew the name of the tree."

The animals cried out, "But who can tell us the name of the tree?"

The very old tortoise answered, "The king knows. We must send someone to ask him."

"I will go," said the gazelle. "I am the fastest runner of us all." And that was true.

So the gazelle started out across the great flat plain. He ran like an arrow shot from a bow, and as he ran he thought, "How lucky the animals are that I am willing to go to the king. No one can run as fast as I."

Indeed, it was not long before the gazelle reached the jungle and the place by the river where the king lived.

The king was sitting with his tail neatly wrapped around him. Every hair in his golden coat lay smooth and shining. He spoke kindly to the gazelle. "What do you wish of me," he said.

"O great king," said the gazelle, "all the animals are hungry and we have found a tree filled with wonderful fruit. But we cannot eat the fruit until we know the name of the tree."

"I will tell you," said the lion, "but you must remember, for I don't want to tell anyone else. The name of the tree is Ungalli."

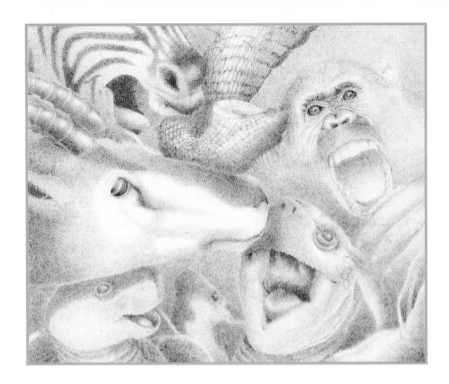

The gazelle thanked the king and began to run through the jungle and across the great flat plain. He thought about how happy all the animals would be, and how they would thank him. He thought about this so hard that he did not see a rabbit hole that lay in his path, not far from where the animals were waiting. He stepped in it and went head over hoofs over hoofs. He landed in a heap at the foot of the tree.

"What is the name of the tree?" shouted the animals.

The gazelle shook his head. But the name was gone. "I can't remember," he whispered.

The animals groaned. "We will have to send someone else," they said. "Someone who will not forget."

"I will go," said the elephant. "I never forget anything."

The animals nodded, for this was true. And so the elephant strode off across the great flat plain.

"I will not forget," she said to herself. "I can remember anything I choose to."

When the elephant arrived at the river, the king was sitting in his usual place, but the end of his tail was twitching and his fur was ruffled.

"What do you want," he growled.

"O king," said the elephant, "all the animals are hungry…"

"I know," said the lion, "and you want to know the name of the tree with the wonderful fruit. I will tell you, but don't forget because I *will not* tell anyone else. The name of the tree is Ungalli."

"I will not forget," said the elephant. "I never forget anything." And she turned and began to make her way out of the jungle.

"Forget," she grumbled to herself. "Me, forget! Why, I can remember the names of all the trees in this jungle." And she began to name them. She was just starting on the trees of the rest of the world when she happened to step in the very same rabbit hole that had tripped the gazelle.

The animals waiting under the tree saw the elephant and ran toward her calling, "What is the name of the tree?"

"I can't remember," she said crossly, "and I don't care. That tree has caused far too much trouble already."

The animals didn't even groan. They were too tired and hungry.

After a long time a very young tortoise spoke. "O animals," he said, "I will go and find out the name of the tree."

"You!" said the animals. "But you are so young and you are so small and you are so slow."

"Yes," said the very young tortoise. "But I know how to remember. I learned from my great-great-great-grandmother, the one who told you about the tree."

The animals had nothing to say. And the little tortoise was already on his way. It is true that he was slow. But by putting one short leg ahead of the other he crossed the great flat plain and arrived at the place by the river where the king lived.

The king was pacing up and down the bank of the river, waving his tail. His fur was standing on end.

When he saw the very young tortoise, he roared, "If you have to come to ask me the name of the tree, go home. I have told the gazelle and I have told the elephant that the name of the tree is Ungalli, and I will *not* tell you."

The very young tortoise nodded his head politely. He turned and began to walk out of the jungle.

As he walked he said, "Uṇgalli, Uṇgalli, the name of the tree is Uṇgalli. Uṇgalli, Uṇgalli, the name of the tree is Uṇgalli."

And he never stopped saying it, even when he got tired, even when he got thirsty. Because that is what his great-great-great-grandmother had told him to do. Even when he fell right to the bottom of that same rabbit hole, the very young tortoise just climbed out saying, "Uṇgalli, Uṇgalli, the name of the tree is Uṇgalli."

None of the animals saw him coming. They were sitting under the tree, looking at the ground. The very young tortoise walked straight up to the foot of the tree and said in a loud voice, "The name of the tree is Ungalli!"

The animals looked up.

They saw the branches of the tree bend down so low that they could reach the wonderful fruit that was red as pomegranates, as yellow as bananas, as green as melons, as purple as plums, and as orange as mangos, and smelled like all the fruits of the world.

The animals ate. They ate until they could eat no more. And then they lifted the very young tortoise high in the air and marched around the tree chanting, "Ungalli, Ungalli, the name of the tree is Ungalli," because they did not want to forget. And they never did.

AFTER YOU READ

Make a chart like this one

Tell what happened at the beginning, the middle, and the end of the story.

What Happened in the Story		
Beginning	**Middle**	**End**

Tell Me a Story

You have read a fairy tale, a fable and a folktale. Think of an idea for a fairy tale of your own that you can tell to the class.

Remember to use fairy tale language like "Once upon a time..."

Plan

Think about your fairy tale with a story map like this.

Who is in the story?

What happened?
1.
2.
3.

How does the story end?

Write your fairy tale

Revise

Think about ways to make your fairy tale better.
- Did you put the events in the right order?
- Does the story make sense?
- Is there anything you should add or take out?

Check

Check your fairy tale for spelling and capitals.

Here's how Simranjeet's story started.

> The Lion and the Princess
> Once upon a time in a far a way land
> there lived a princess named Hannah.
> She found a lion named Fuzzy. She
> played with Fuzzy a lot. One day Fuzzy
> could not find Hannah. He searched
> and searched. But he could not find
> Hannah. She was on her way to
> England. It was very far for a lion.

Practise

- Read aloud in a strong, slow voice.
- Use different voices for different parts.
- Read it to show the how the characters feel.

Share

Share your story
by reading it aloud
to the class.

Read it into a
tape recorder
to hear what it
sounds like.

ACKNOWLEDGMENTS

Permission to reprint copyrighted material is gratefully acknowledged. Every effort has been made to trace ownership of all copyrighted material and to secure permission from copyright holders. In the event of any question arising as to the use of any material, we will be pleased to make the necessary corrections in future printings.

"I Am" from IT'S RAINING LAUGHTER by Nikki Grimes. Copyright © 1997 by Nikki Grimes. Used by permission of Dial Books for Young Readers, a division of Penguin Putnam Inc. "What's Your Name?" text copyright © 1995 by Eve Sanders. Photographs (pp. 9-11) copyright © 1995 by Marilyn Sanders. All rights reserved. Reprinted from WHAT'S YOUR NAME? By permission of Holiday House, Inc. "The Leaving Morning" from The Leaving Morning by Angela Johnson, illustrated by David Soman. Text © 1992 by Angela Johnson. Illustrations © 1992 by David Soman. Reprinted by permission of Orchard Books, New York. "Violet's Purple World" © 1999 John McLaughlin. Alexander and the Terrible, Horrible, No Good, Very Bad Day by Judith Viorst. Text copyright © 1972 by Judith Viorst. Illustrations copyright © 1972 by Ray Cruz. Reprinted with permission of Atheneum Books for Young Readers, Simon & Schuster Children's Publishing Division. "Advertise It!" by Mark Cressman © 1999 ITP Nelson. "Postcard Messages" text © 1997 Linda Granfield from the book Postcards Talk. Reprinted with permission. Pembroke Publishers, 538 Hood Road, Markham, Ontario L3R 3K9. "Pictures Talk" by Susan Green © 1999 ITP Nelson. "In the News" by Robert Cutting © 1999 ITP Nelson. "The Gifts of Spring" by Jan Bourdeau Waboose. Reprinted with permission of the author. "Window Watcher" adapted from QUICK-AND-EASY Learning Centers: SCIENCE by Lynne Kepler, published by Scholastic Professional Books. Copyright © 1995 by Scholastic Inc. Reproduced by permission. "The Great Swamp" by Kiera Schneider from WILD Magazine, June/July 1998 published by Malcolm Publishing Inc. Reproduced with permission of author. "What Good is a Swamp?" from WILD Magazine, June/July 1998 published by Malcolm Publishing Inc. Reproduced with permission. "Frog Time" by Sue Ann Alderson from Pondseasons. Text copyright © 1997 by Sue Ann Alderson. Illustrations copyright © 1997 by Ann Blades. A Groundwood Book/Douglas & McIntyre.

"Salamander Room" text copyright © 1991 by Anne Mazer. Illustrations copyright © 1991 by Steve Johnson and Lou Fancher. Reproduced with permission of Random House, Inc. "Make a Terrarium" by Lizann Flatt © 1999 ITP Nelson. THIS LAND IS YOUR LAND. Words and Music by Woody Guthrie. Canadian lyrics by The Travellers. TRO © Copyright 1956 (Renewed) 1958 (Renewed) 1970 (Renewed) Ludlow Music, Inc., New York, New York. Used by permission. The Fable of the Three Frogs collected by Carole Spray. Reproduced with permission of Carole Spray. "The Name of the Tree" abridged and adapted from The Name of the Tree. Text copyright © 1989 by Celia Barker Lottridge. Illustrations copyright © 1989 by Ian Wallace. A Groundwood Book/ Douglas & McIntyre.

Illustrations

Cover: Sharon Matthews; p. 6 (top) Lynn Jeffery, (bottom) David Soman; p. 7 (top) Dusan Petricic, (bottom) Ray Cruz; pp. 14-19 David Soman; pp. 20-29 Lynn Jeffery; pp. 32-43 Ray Cruz; pp. 44-45 Tina Holdcroft; pp. 46-47 Norman Eyolfson; pp. 48-55 Ann Iosa; pp. 61-63 Capucine Mazille; pp. 64-65 Tina Holdcroft; pp. 66-67 Eric Copeland; pp. 68-71 Stephen Quinlan; pp. 78-81 Steve Attoe; pp. 82-83 Ann Blades; pp. 84-91 Steve Johnson and Lou Fancher; pp. 92-95 Bart Vallecoccia; pp. 96-97 Tina Holdcroft; pp. 98-99 Susan Todd; pp. 100-107 Blanche Sims; pp. 108-111 Joe Weissmann; pp. 112-125 Ian Wallace; pp. 126-127 Tina Holdcroft

Photographs

pp. 7, 9-11 © Marilyn Sanders; p. 12 courtesy of Bonnie Miller; p.13 courtesy of Carolyn Porteous; p. 30 (top left) © Walter Bibikow/The Image Bank, (top right) © Robert E Daemmrich/Tony Stone Images, (bottom left) © PhotoDisc, Inc, (bottom right) © Roger Charity/Tony Stone Images; p. 31 (top left) © Ottmar Bierwagen/Ivy Images, (top right) Dave Starrett, (bottom left) © Don Klumpp/The Image Bank, (bottom right) © David Young-Wolff/Tony Stone Images; p. 56 courtesy of The Toronto Sun; p. 57 © Lori Adamski Peek/Tony Stone Images; p. 58 (top) © Gary Cralle/The Image Bank, (bottom) © Corel Corporation; p. 59 courtesy of The Toronto Star; p. 72 courtesy of Dan Schneider; p. 73 © Randy Wells/Tony Stone Images; p. 74 courtesy of Dan Schneider; p. 75 © Tony Arruza/Tony Stone Images; p. 76 © PhotoDisc, Inc; p. 77 © David Muench/Tony Stone Images